BLUE-PRINT

tO

SELF-ESTEEM

(OLDER GIRL EDITION)

"For we are God's handiwork"

Ephesians 2:10

By: Keisha Montfleury

Blueprint to Self Esteem

(Older Girl Edition)

By Keisha Montfleury

Copyright 2019 by Keisha Montfleury

This book is dedicated to all my *OG'S* (Older Girls)

please remember and always know that:

"YOU ARE GOD'S HANDIWORK"

I wanna THANK YOU so much for taking the time to read this book! Whether you picked it up on your own, or it was given to you by your mother, older sister, mentor or coach, it is NOT BY ACCIDENT that you have this book. I prayed for each and every girl that will read this book and take the time to do the activities that are specifically designed for you to grow into the young woman that GOD is ultimately calling you to become.

I want you to know that this book is for my girls that may be battling with things like a low self-esteem or anxiety AND for my girls that feel as though she already have a high self-esteem or is already confident within herself; we all can benefit from being poured into, and that is what I am here for, **TO PLANT THE SEEDS OF ENCOURAGEMENT** to you ladies. I believe that wherever you are in your journey, this book will support you in that.

I want to first start off with letting you know of 3 things (if you don't get anything else from this book, PLEASE, PLEASE, PLEASE remember these 3 things...ok are you ready? Here goes!

1. **THE MOST IMPORTANT RELATIONSHIP YOU WILL HAVE IS THE ONE THAT YOU WILL HAVE WITH GOD, HE will walk you through the girl, young lady, and ultimately the woman HE is calling you to become. HE will guide you through the process and the journey of your PURPOSE**

2. The second most important relationship is the one you will have with yourself; you will always need to make sure that you are caring for, investing in, and valuing yourself. This will set you up to have healthy boundaries for yourself and others, capture any red flags (I use the term RED BANNERS; banners are bigger, and people will most likely show you who they are from the very beginning, it's just on us to make the decision on what we are willing to accept or not). This will also set you up to have standards for yourself and others in your life.

3. AND LAST BUT NOT LEAST IS THAT ALL OF THIS TAKES PRACTICE!!!

I really want you to remember that, because you (we) are human beings, are NOT perfect and you are going to make mistakes, but it's ok. Now I don't want you to purposefully make mistakes, but I do want you to learn from the one's you make and seek out support from other women and resources that you are comfortable with.

This book is meant to be used as one of those resources, it is meant for you to be able to grow into the knowledge, tools, and strategies to thrive as individuals.

Why am I doing this and why is this important to me? Well I am glad that you asked.

I myself participated in unhealthy relationships due to having a low-self- esteem, it wasn't until GOD captured my heart and started guiding me through the woman HE is calling me to become, letting me know that MY PURPOSE is to encourage girls like yourself to have a HEALTHY CONFIDENCE and to know your worth through Christ, so that you can change the world in the way HE has called you to.

So I want you to know that I am practicing these skills myself, and the truth is some days may be tough, but remember that you always have resources around you that can support you in the way that you need it!

Before we get started, I also want to make sure that you know important words that you will see all throughout this book along with the **5 Keys of a Healthy Confidence**,

(they will each be explained more thoroughly in the following pages):

- **Purpose**
- **Self-Care**
- **Journey**
- **Health and Nutrition**
- **Investment**

Some of the other words that I use often that you will see throughout are:

- **Abundantly- a lot of, large amount, plenty**
- **Authentic- genuine, real, honest, dependable**

- Beauty-FULL- gorgeous, charming, delightful, lovely
- Oohh La La- surprised with someone's beauty

(this is what happens when you practice self-care)

- Mindful-taking time for what matters
- Volunteer-participate freely
- Gift- something willingly given to someone without payment; a present
- Skill- the ability to do something well

PURPOSE

pur·pose

/'pərpəs/

the reason for which something is done or created or for which something exists.

Some synonyms include motive, motivation, cause, reason

I am here to tell you that

YOU HAVE A PURPOSE

Did you know that WE ALL HAVE A PURPOSE? God has created each and every one of us to something specific in this world. We are supposed to be making a difference by using our gifts, talents, and skills to serve other people.

You are probably wondering

"Serve?"

"What do you mean by that?"

Well, in the bible **Ephesians 2:10** says *For we are God's handiwork created in Christ Jesus to do good works which HE already prepared us in advance to do.*

That means that God has already prepared you in advance to do what you were meant to do!

Are you wondering what that is?

Well I am glad that you asked! In the next few pages there will be a small questionnaire that will help you get started on your journey to figuring out what your gifts, talents, and skills are.

**this questionnaire is just meant to get you to start thinking. Even though it is meant to help you narrow down your interests, I want you to remember that your interests may change over time.

**You can also ask people closest to you, to help you answer some of the questions, sometimes the people closest to us can see things about ourselves that we can overlook.

Gifts, Talents, and Purpose

A gift something that comes natural to you. What are your gifts?

1.

2.

3.

What skills do you have that separate you from everyone else?

1.

2.

3.

What sparks your interest?

1.

2.

3.

What activities do you do that can make you forget to eat, go to the bathroom?

1.

2.

3.

If you got to write your own book, what would it be about?

1.

2.

3.

What kinds of topics do you love to talk to others about?

1.

2.

3.

What would you be interested in getting paid to do?

1.

2.

3.

What activities interests you, that you can't imagine living without?

1.

2.

3.

Now look at all of your interests, talents, and gifts and see what pops out to you!

Self-Care

/ˌselfˈker/

the practice of taking an active role in protecting one's own
well-being and happiness

IT IS IMPORTANT TO CARE FOR YOURSELF

Self-Care is a popular topic to talk about now a day. Even though it is super important for you ladies to practice self-care, I want to make sure that you ladies understand why it is important and how to create a self-care routine for yourself. Your routine will not look like someone else's, it will be unique to you.

I want to let you know right off the bat, that taking care of your body is something that you should desire to do and should be practicing. So, making sure that you do things like taking showers or baths on a regular basis, combing your hair and trying new hair styles, putting lotion on your skin, Chapstick, or lip gloss on your lips...all of this is very necessary. We don't want to ever become obsessed with ourselves, but we do want to be mindful with caring for our bodies.

Here are some ideas that you can do to practice self-care. You will also write out 3 ways that you will intentionally practice your self-care routine that you chose. Enjoy!

Here is a cool recipe for you to start caring for your skin:

Sugar Scrub Ingredients

1. 1/2 cup sugar (white or brown sugar-preferably organic)

2. 1/2 cup oil (olive oil and coconut oil work great)

3. Optional: essential oils of your preference

10 Simple Ways to Practice Self-Care

1. Eat healthily and mindfully.

Too often we eat our meals while multitasking, thus denying ourselves the pure experience of nourishing meal. Would you work on the computer when having dinner with a loved one? Treat yourself with that same level of respect and allow yourself to indulge in a meal without any distractions.

2. Keep track of your accomplishments.

While there are great merits to a "to-do" list, we must also recognize the things we've done. At the end of the day, make a list (either mental or write it out) of the productive things you've done that day. Did you nurture a relationship? Do the laundry? Complete a work assignment? No matter how small, you deserve a pat on the back.

3. Express gratitude.

Just as it's beneficial to keep track of what we've done, it's also good to notice what we have. Keep a journal by your bed and note the things that you feel lucky to have. Everything from clean sheets to a good friend is worth noting.

4. Gift your inner child.

What were some of your favorite things when you were little? Did you love sidewalk chalk, picking wildflowers, or eating marshmallows? Treat your inner child to a little present and allow the warm feelings to wash over you.

5. Create a cozy space.

Does your bedroom look the way you want it to? If it doesn't, maybe add some candles or fun throw pillows. By building a space that feels warm and inviting, you establish an inviting retreat for when tough times arise.

6. Read a book.

Finding a book, you love is a great way to feel happy. It feels wonderful to look forward to a good story, and the act of reading helps encourage a sense of peace.

7. Move.

What people say about exercise and endorphins is true; getting active **increases feelings of happiness**. This doesn't mean you need to hit the gym. Rather find a form of physical activity that works for you. Go dancing with your friends, enjoy a Saturday morning hike, or go on a bike ride.

8. Unplug.

Instagram and Facebook have some benefits, but does it really make you feel better to expose yourself to everyone's online versions of themselves? Most often people only report on their success, and so **it can be hard** when you're comparing your entire life to everyone's highlight reels. Take the time to break away from social media and allow yourself to focus on the beauty of the moment.

9. Create something.

Whether it's a batch of brownies or a pastel drawing, getting artistic allows us to feel mindful and productive.

10. Build a self-care kit.

Fill a pretty basket with some of the things that make you feel special. It could be nail polish, gummy frogs, coconut lotion, treasured photos, or a new pair of socks. Place your pick-me-ups in a pretty basket and keep it in your bedroom or bathroom for when you need an extra dose of love.

Remember, by being your best self you're able to share those beautiful feelings with those around you. Search for the good, share your peace, and watch the positivity grow.

What are some ways you are going to practice

SELF-CARE?

My Favorite Self-Care Ideas
1.
2.
3.

JOURNEY

jour·ney

/ˈjərnē/

an act of traveling from one place to another

Synonyms include voyage, trip, cruise, transfer, wandering

Did you get to look at the definition of JOURNEY? If you really take a look at it, it may say to travel from one place to another, but for me I want to open your eyes to letting you know that in this book it does not just mean traveling from place to place. Journey (in this book) is to let you know that **YOU ARE ON A JOURNEY**. Your life is a JOURNEY! And just like I explained earlier you have a PURPOSE to fulfill in this world. Life may be challenging at times, but I want you to know that it will pass. Take the time to enjoy what you can about your life, enjoy the little things, be grateful for the big things, look forward to your future, but make sure that you are enjoying your present.

I would like to ask you what things are you looking
forward to, in your JOURNEY of life?

_____

_____

_____

_____

_____

_____

_____

_____

Along with your life being a JOURNEY, I would like you to think about two more things when I talk about journey:

Exercising and Traveling

Before you start to get overwhelmed with the thought of exercising, I am going to share with you easy ways that you can get started. You will come up with a small exercise routine that is meant to make sure that you are being intentional with exercising your body. Some of the benefits of exercising are not only for you to lose weight (which would be good right?), but it also helps you to feel better, and boosts up your energy for the day. Some ways that you can exercise naturally or in a fun way are:

- Swimming
- Walking around the block with friends
- Roller skating
- Jogging
- Riding your bike
- Playing an active video game

I want you to start thinking of some ways that you can exercise your body, and write it down below, along with when you will exercise and who you can ask to exercise with you.

My exercise routine

1. Choose 1 day of the week to exercise? And what activity will you do?

2. Choose the time you will do this? And for how long

3. Who will you exercise with? (or who will you ask to hold you accountable?)

Traveling (and having the desire to travel) is something that is important for us also. There are so many beautiful people and things in this world, so much sight to see.

Let me ask you one question.

"If I gave you a plane ticket to go anywhere in the world, where would you go?"

Here is a map of the United States *but please keep in mind that there is a whole world out there so I encourage you to look at the world map (you can google this), and just use your imagination!

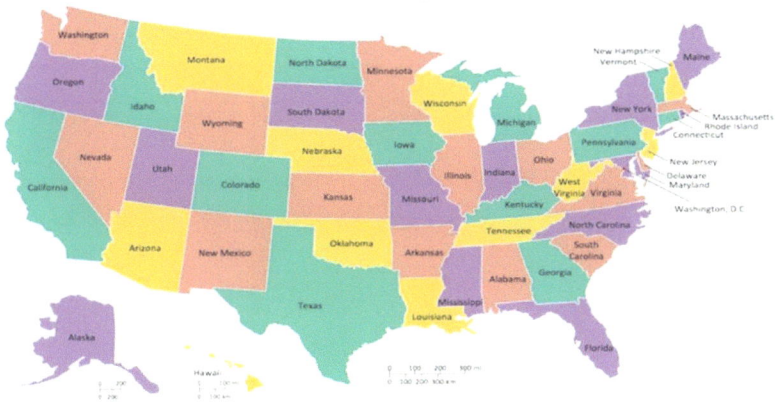

My travel desires
1.
2.
3.

Health & Nutrition

MATTERS

Your HEALTH & NUTRITION does MATTER! The way that you nourish yourself is important. Don't worry, I am not going to get on you about your eating habits (well not too much) or try to get you to go vegan or vegetarian.

I just want to share with you how important it is that you are being mindful with the things that you are putting inside of your bodies. It is ok to eat your favorite foods, but out of everything that you will read in this section I want to make sure that you remember that everything that you do should be done in moderation.

In the next few pages I will share some information with you a couple of recipes for you that you will be able to easily do with little effort.

Different Types of Lettuce:

(and their benefits)

Kale

- o   Has a ruffled edge
- o   Comes in a variety of colors
- o   33 calories per serving
- o   serving size is 1 cup

Romaine

- o   crispier than many leafy greens
- o   8 calories per serving
- o   serving size is 1 cup
- o   good source of dietary fiber, vitamins A, C, K, Thiamin, Folate, Iron, Potassium and Manganese

Spinach

- good source of
- 7 calories per serving
- serving size is 1 cup
- 987% of DV for vitamin K
- good source of antioxidants

Additional Tips

- The darker the healthier – that means that read leaf is a little healthier than green
- The serving size for leafy greens is between one cup (about the size of half a baseball) and half a cup

Fruits and their Benefits:

Lemons:

Researchers believe that the flavonoids in lemon and other citrus fruits have antibacterial, anticancer, and antidiabetic properties.

Strawberries:

They contain anthocyanins, which are flavonoids that can help boost heart health. The fiber and potassium in strawberries can also support a healthy heart.

Oranges:

The human body cannot make vitamin C itself, so people need to get this vitamin from their diet. Oranges also contain high levels of pectin, which is a fiber that can keep the colon healthy by binding to chemicals that can cause cancer and removing them from the colon.

Limes:

Limes are a sour citrus fruit that provide a range of health benefits. Like other citrus fruits, limes provide a healthful dose of vitamin C. They also have similar health benefits, antibacterial, and antioxidant properties.

Grapefruit:

The flavonoids in grapefruits can help protect against some cancers, inflammation, and obesity

A Couple of Vegan Recipes

<u>Recipe 1:</u>
Puttanesca

Spaghetti noodle or whatever thin pasta you want.
• olives • fresh basil • salt and pepper
• fresh garlic • grape tomatoes • olive oil •
tomato sauce of choice

Boil noodles.
Once completed drain water.
In a separate pan, pan cook all ingredients
except fresh basil for about 10 minutes.

Once completed, add noodles to pan of sauce,
mix well.

Serve immediately and top with chopped fresh
basil.
Feel free to add a vegan shredded mozzarella if
you want.
Enjoy.

__Recipe 2__
Quick breakfast

1 bagel split and toasted.
In a bowl mix 1 avocado with pepper,
nutritional yeast, chia seeds, and little Ms. Dash
seasoning.

Mix together.

Spread on toasted bagel with slices of tomato
and viola

Then adding a vegan slice of deli meat or vegan
cheese in addition to make a sandwich.

Breakfast is served.

INVESTMENT

in·vest·ment
/in'ves(t)mənt/

The act of devoting time, effort, or energy to a undertaking
with the expectation of a worthwhile result

Investing in others is what we should strive to do, be intentional, be grateful, be mindful be you!

When you hear the word "investment" your probably think about money. While yes that is a part of investing, but there are other ways of investing that I would like to share with you.

One way is making sure that you are making the time to take care of yourself (there are plenty of ways to do that, as you have been reading in this book); another way is to make sure that you are making the time to connect with other people in your life, meaning spending time with your best friends, your mom, dad, or other family members.

Another way of investing is to make sure that you are making the time to volunteer, and not just volunteer anywhere, but volunteer at places and organizations that have meaning to you, and that you care about.

3 People I will spend more time with
1.
2.
3.

Does the thought of caring for animals pull at your heart? Do you have an interest for caring for children? What about the homeless, do you have ideas on how to help and support them? Well these things are in your heart for a reason, and when you are volunteering your time you can start with what your interests are, and go out of your way to serve them (something as little as a couple of hours a month, can make a big difference). I want you to think about these places and write them down below.

3 Places I can volunteer
1.
2.
3.

Oh and last but not least, how you are thinking about investing your money is important! Did you think I would not bring that up? LOL

Some of you may have a job or are thinking about getting a job. That is good, that means that you may be ready for responsibility! I am just going to use this time to suggest to you, that when you start working you want to get into the habit of doing these three things with your money:

1.   Tithe 10%
2.   Save 10%
3.   Budget the rest

If you get into the habit of budgeting your money now, then it won't be so hard when as you get older or are making more money.

Remember in the beginning of the book where I said that the number one relationship you will have is the one that you have with GOD? Well tithing is one of the ways that you show GOD that you are being a good steward with your money. Don't get it twisted, GOD does not need your money, HE just wants you to learn how to be disciplined and this is a way to make sure that you are giving back to your community. Don't be forced to tithe to a certain place or church. Just get into the habit of making sure that 10% of your money goes to an organization of your choice that you are passionate about.

You also want to make sure that you get into the habit of saving 10% of your money. This money is saved and is not supposed to be touched. Try and start saving for something that you really want, but just get into the habit of having some of your money saved up for emergencies and for goals that you would like to reach.

3 Places I will consider TITHING to

1.

2.

3.

3 things that I will have to save up for

1.

2.

3.

As we wrap it all up, and get ready to leave, I want to make sure that you BELIVE that you are very capable of practicing EVERYTHING that was outlined in this book. I BELIEVE IN YOU, and I know for a fact that GOD has a purpose for your life (and if you didn't know, or no one has ever told you that) THEN YOU ARE HEARING IT NOW!! LOL

So let's get started girl!

Get up!

Today is the day that you will start to WALK CONFIDENLY INTO YOUR PURPOSE!

I want to make sure that we end with the same way that we began...remembering THREE things:

1.   The MOST IMPORTANT RELATIONSHIP YOU WILL HAVE IS THE ONE THAT YOU WILL HAVE WITH GOD. HE will walk you through the girl, the young lady, and ultimately the woman HE is calling you to become.
2.   The second most important relationship you will have is the one you have with yourself, you will always need to be caring for, investing in, and valuing yourself, this will set you up to have healthy relationships with other people in your life
3.   Last but not least, THIS ALL TAKES PRACTICE

Here are a few scriptures from the bible that is useful to help you remember what GOD says about you (me) (us).

Ephesians 2:10 For we are GOD'S handiwork, created in Christ Jesus to do good works he already prepared us in advance to do

John 15:15 I am a friend of Christ

Romans 8:37 I am more than a conqueror through Christ

2 Corinthians 5:17 I am a new creation

John 1:12 I am a child of God

Philippians 4:13 I am able to do all things through Christ who strengthens me

John 17:13 I am filled with Christ's joy

1 Thessalonians 1:4 I am chosen by God

My intention for sharing these scriptures with you is to let you know what GOD says about you! So if anyone ever tells you the opposite of what HIS words says about you, then you know that is a lie, and not to believe those lies. *And guess what sometimes the very person who is telling you negative stuff about you, IS YOU! We must be very careful with the things that we are saying about our own selves. So, keep these scriptures (truths) near you always, write them down, and repeat them on a consistent basis if you have to.

Another thing that I want to make sure that I leave you with is a space to be able to journal and/or write your thoughts and prayers out to God.

*Some of you are probably wondering "how do I talk to God?" or "I never prayed before, so how do I do that?"

Well I am so glad that you asked.

Talking to God is just like talking to a trusted friend, but better! Praying to God is just talking to HIM. Letting HIM know what's going on in your life (*hint* HE already know, since HE knows everything), but just like you would make the time to talk to your best friend, you should make the time to talk to GOD. And when you talk to HIM make sure it is coming from a pure heart, and that you are being open to what HE wants to share with you. Thank HIM first for all that HE has blessed you with (your life, your family, your health, your purpose, etc.), and wait to listen to what He has to say to you (*another hint...sometimes HIS answer may be quick, or it may take a little time) just be patient.

Below you will find a space to journal/write your thoughts and prayers.

Well I hope and pray that you found this book useful! Thank you for taking the time to read it and remember girl that you are **GOD'S HANDIWORK!!**

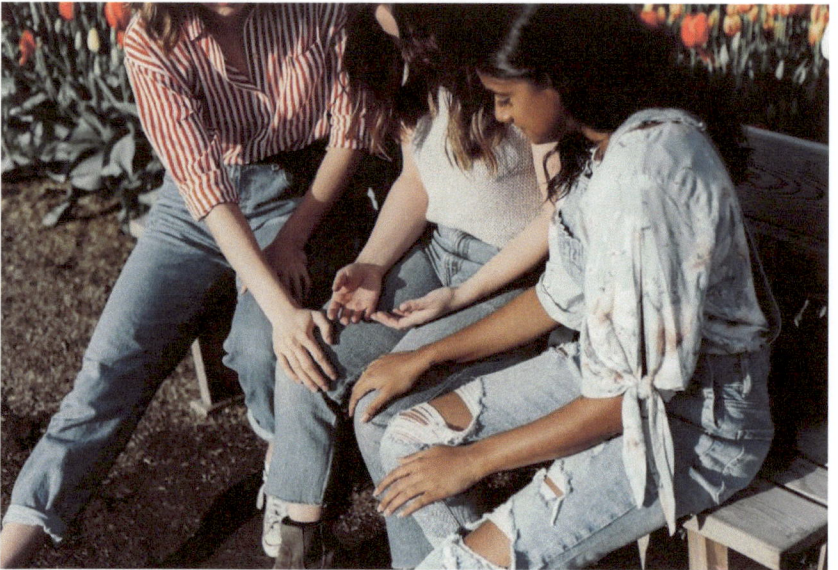

Notes and Prayers:

Notes and Prayers:

Notes and Prayers:

Notes and Prayers:

Notes and Prayers:

Notes and Prayers:

Notes and Prayers:

Notes and Prayers:

www.ingramcontent.com/pod-product-compliance
Lightning Source LLC
LaVergne TN
LVHW010031070426
835508LV00005B/299